Hillary's Story

A Story of Selflessness, Commitment, and Unconditional Love

Christine Harrod Walker

To Hillary and Brandon
for sharing their dream
so that I could fulfill
one of my own.

"Fairy Tales can come true,
it can happen to you"

"Young at Heart" Song by Frank Sinatra

Released 1953

Music by Johnny Richards,

Lyrics by Carolyn Leigh

Contents

1.

I Had Mail

He picked me. Before the great techno wizards conjured up the endless opportunities the Internet would bring, and before the sages dreamed the soul-mate connections that online match-making services would create, and long before the movie *You've Got Mail* appeared, *I* had mail. I had "Intranet" at Utah State University.

It was 1994, and USU's Intranet service connected students to their professors and to each other and had begun to pioneer the advancement of e-mail. It would change the world—mine included.

2.

My Early Years

I was the first of four daughters. Since I didn't come with a parenting manual, I was the practice run for the other three. I never had to think for myself, as my parents were eager and ready to think for me. Practicing on me helped them to write the manual for their next three.

My family is loving and kind and we have a close relationship. I had a pretty normal childhood and we were much more fortunate than lots of other families.

We lived in Virginia, where my father worked on nuclear power plants. He got his formal education at Utah State University. Logan, Utah, would remain home to him. It wasn't home to any of the rest of my family. I never thought it would ever become mine.

After graduating from a Virginia high school, I tried college at Utah State University—my dad's alma mater.

My stay was brief but life changing. I had no direction and spent my time being rebellious. I enjoyed being in charge of my life, even though I had no purpose. I liked making my own decisions, even if they were wrong. I was too busy having fun to bother with the education part of college. It didn't take long, about a year, for my parents to reel me in and bring me back home to rethink my situation.

Then Chernobyl happened, half a world away. My dad's position working on the Virginia nuclear power plant was suddenly gone.   My family packed up and prepared to move to Venezuela, of all places, where my dad would oversee the building and expansion of an existing refinery.

We had moved time and time again for my dad's career. We were survivors. My dad's two tours of duty in Vietnam as a tank retriever gave him the confidence to move forward no matter what. I learned that important lesson from him.

My mother took over as the primary breadwinner whenever necessary. She took on many jobs. She sold real estate, made draperies, worked for a packing company, and worked in a culinary store. She was also teaching us life lessons.

We were not a religious family and we did not attend a church. I really hadn't thought about religion that much. It wasn't a part of our lives.

While I was at Utah State, I met students who witnessed their faith and their path and what they believe. I was curious. I loved how their faith gave them strength and purpose. They talked openly about the spirit. Who or what was this spirit that they spoke of when they witnessed?

I reluctantly went back to Virginia, but had this nagging feeling that I shouldn't have left. I was trying to sort out this "faith" concept and what it might mean for me. Something was luring me back to Utah. I knew if I returned, I would meet someone that was going to change my life. I could not explain or ignore this burning certainty. I had to try it once more.

I headed back to Utah to try again. I rented a second-floor apartment with three other girls. Decked out in 1970's avocado green, the apartment had a peculiar smell to match. I avoided looking too closely into corners or underneath cabinets. The four of us shared a bathroom and the germs that I am sure were in it. It certainly wasn't home sweet home, and we were certainly not a family. We shared an apartment, and that was the extent of it. In spite of the less –than- perfect situation, however, I was glad to be back in school. I didn't know why, but I knew it was the place for me to be.

3.

Finding Direction

After settling into Utah the second time, I remember lying awake one night, tossing and turning, and just staring at the ceiling. I suddenly realized that my thoughts were prayers, and that I was pouring out my feelings and hoping there was someone waiting to hear my plea. Was there someone listening? I desperately needed to know. I wanted purpose. Where was I going? It was so overwhelming to me to think that others could actually answer that question. They lived and breathed their faith.

When I got up the next morning, I felt somehow different than I had the night before. I felt a euphoria that I had never known. I even felt centered and like everything would be all right. I went looking for friends in a near by dorm to find out what had happened to me. They were so glad to tell me about the Spirit of Christ and how I had found it. Was that because of my prayer? I wondered if I had found the Spirit of Christ, or did He find me? I needed answers.

They invited me to go to the first-of-the-month fast and testimony meeting at their Stake House. I was living in the college ward, so the meeting was filled with college students and missionaries, pouring out their hearts and witnessing their knowledge of the Gospel. I was amazed at how sure they were. They knew their faith. After witnessing all of this, I needed to seek help immediately. I ran back to the dorm to look for the missionaries. When I opened the door, there they were, waiting for me. I didn't have to look for them, they were led to me.

I was like a sponge soaking up their words. They taught me to pray. My friends and I sat in a circle in my room and read the Book of Mormon. We each took a chapter and went around in the circle until we had read the entire book in one night. They challenged me to be baptized.

I called my parents, who had no knowledge of what was going on in my life. I told them the story of finding faith and direction, and I told them that I wanted to be baptized. They said that I should think seriously about what I was going to do. I told them that I would wait a while before I did anything.

But I just couldn't wait. I felt so strongly that I needed to be baptized. At a family home evening gathering, I met a young man from the same small town in Virginia where I had lived. He was the person designated to confirm me in the faith. I was baptized by one of the missionaries. To them, I was a "golden" convert. I was so ready and willing. I really didn't know where all this would lead me, but I was sure it was the right path. I was a new member of the Church of Jesus Christ of Latter-day Saints. I had direction.

4.

Brandon's Plea

While I had been searching for truth and was eventually baptized into the LDS faith, Brandon had been praying faithfully for a true friend. He wanted to share his life with a girl and knew together they would have a wonderful life and he would never again be lonely. A few weeks after school had resumed, he said another prayer asking for guidance. From his home computer, he pulled up the list of students that were online. He carefully navigated the list and was inspired to stop at my name. He picked me. I was in the college library, linked into the Intranet network. And just like that, I had mail from Brandon Thornley.

The first message simply said, "Can I tell you a story?" When I responded in the affirmative, he began telling me about a boy who had spent his life in a wheelchair. The boy's life was pretty normal up until the age of fourteen months, at which time, things started to change. While the little boy had learned to sit up, he needed his legs bent behind him for support. His parents noticed that it wasn't a normal posture for a developing child. The little boy's parents didn't want to admit that there was something wrong, but soon, it was undeniable.

There were countless questions and never-ending visits to doctors until all hope of normalcy was gone—not what a young couple wants to hear about their first-born child. The diagnosis was a rare form of muscular dystrophy called spinal muscular atrophy. Not only would his physical development cease, they were told, but he wasn't supposed to live beyond four years of age. The disease isn't researched or funded because the life expectancy is so short. He would never stand on his own. He would never walk. He would have limited use of his arms. All the dreams his parents had had for their little boy were gone. "That little boy," he concluded in his e-mail, "was me."

I couldn't believe what I was reading. I soaked in every word and feeling conveyed. He poured out his soul in this message. It was a cry for help. While campus life was convening, and students were eager to begin the new semester, Brandon's life hadn't changed—not in a long time—and he worried that his life would forever be the same.

He lived at home with his parents in a room that was an office they'd converted into a bedroom. They had recently moved from Smithfield to Logan to make college more accessible to him. It was accessible, but he certainly wasn't living the *real* college life.

Until this point, he had lived his life fearlessly, yet he worried that he would be dependent upon his parents forever. He needed a confidant. He had many friends and relationships, but no one person with whom to share his innermost thoughts and concerns. He wanted a special girl, of his LDS faith, who would become his friend. He could accept that his life would be lived in a wheelchair, but he could not accept that his life would be lived alone.

Reading his words, tears filled my eyes, and I knew that the lump in my throat wasn't going to go away anytime soon. I was just thankful that I didn't have to speak. With this one message, I knew him. And I needed to know more.

I counted the minutes every day until I could go to the library to see if Brandon was online. I couldn't wait to get there. We chatted every day. He told me more about his life. We were both first born, we each had three sisters, and each one of us had a sister named Tiffany. We were from the same faith, though he was raised in it, and I had just begun my journey. We were born fifteen days apart.

Each cyber meeting uncovered something new. He had been a happy child. He was named the poster child in his community for muscular dystrophy in 1980. He loved elementary school and didn't encounter problems until middle school. He became a target then and was always a captive audience. He was shoved into rooms, rolled into the girls' bathroom, and pushed into corners and underwent all other creative forms of humiliation that kids could dream up. Some kid even tried to push him in his wheelchair down the stairs. He was the only student that couldn't fight back. He even had a teacher that locked him outside the classroom and told him he couldn't come in until he could do it by himself.

5.

Face-to-Face

I felt his faith. He had learned at an early age that fear would do him no good, although he had good reason to fear. He needed the generosity of others every day. He needed the hands and feet of other people to take over when he couldn't. He had always relied on God and chose faith over fear. His attitude was contagious. I could see how he had the ability to lift the spirits of others. He faced every day with hope and courage and knew that God would never lead him to a place where He wasn't present. Fear was disabling, and Brandon didn't need another disability.

We had been writing back and forth for several weeks. Eventually, it was time to take our friendship to the next level: it was time to meet.

Logistically, it was easier for me to go to him. I drove to his house, and the entire time I wondered what I was doing. I felt the flutters of anxiety brewing. It was a lot like having a blind date. I felt I knew him already. All I was really doing was putting a face to his name. Wasn't I just trying to rationalize all of this? Even though I knew he was disabled, I hadn't seen him in a wheelchair. The reality of it all was overwhelming.

His room had an outside entrance. I knocked and went inside. Neither of us said a word for a moment. We just looked at each other. Brandon finally broke the silence. "You are even more beautiful than I had dreamed." He had a wonderful smile and sense of confidence. He was cute, and somehow I hadn't expected that. He asked me to sit next to him.

I was surprised at his confidence. Why did I think that a person in a wheelchair would have low self-esteem? I guess I'd been buying into a stereotype about disabilities without realizing it. Brandon was witty, intelligent, honest, loyal, faithful, attractive, kind, easy to talk to—and had to get around in a wheelchair. Why would one negative cancel out all those positive attributes? Why did I think that living in a wheelchair was only a negative?

Our first visit was short—maybe because I was constantly choking back tears. He was so comforting and patient. He knew my reaction well, because he had seen it many times in his life. People would meet him and then have to sort through their feelings about his disability. He held my hand and comforted me with his words.

Coming face-to-face with him and his wheelchair made me sad for him and the things he wasn't able to do. I could feel some of the struggle he had endured. I hurt for him.

He had worried about how I might react. He had experienced that in an earlier relationship. He realized that his previous girlfriend wasn't able to get past the wheelchair. Before meeting him, I'd subconsciously categorized his life as somehow "less" because of the wheelchair. Now, I left so confused.

I knew we had strong feelings for one another already. I knew that the very first moment I'd walked through his door, even though neither of us had expressed it. I knew I wanted him in my life. I just didn't know how this would work.

The second meeting was better. I couldn't wait to see him. We were so used to talking to one another on the computer that I needed to reconnect with those earlier feelings. He gave me his full attention and was ever present no matter how silly the conversation. His eyes never left mine. He knew I would have things to sort out about this relationship. It was worth the work. My life had drastically changed, and I could never go back. It was way too late.

6.

Dating Brandon

Brandon wanted so badly to take me on a date. In a wheelchair, though, even simple outings can be difficult. But getting around in the real world was nothing new for Brandon. He was well aware of the difficulties, but it wasn't impossible. With a little extra planning, he made it a wonderful evening.

The anticipation is always a part of the excitement, and I couldn't contain mine. I must have tried on and taken off a half dozen different outfits. I wanted to look perfect. I obsessed over my hair and makeup. I fidgeted with everything. Shoes and handbag had to go with my dress. Perfume needed to be a scent that would linger in his memory. I wanted to get it right. After all, Brandon was trying to get everything right. The important part was that he would find a way for us to be together..

Brandon would need a vehicle that allowed for a wheelchair. He would use the family van. He then asked a friend to go on a double date with us so that I could enjoy the date without having to worry about Brandon's needs. Brandon couldn't drive, so he asked his friend if he would. I sat by Brandon in the back. We were all nervous. But thanks to Brandon's careful planning, the evening went off without a hitch.

He thought of everything. First he acquired Boyz 2 Men tickets, and then he worked out the logistics. He brought me roses. We all had dinner at the Spaghetti Factory. Even eating is harder for Brandon. His fine motor skills aren't as developed. It takes him much longer than most people to eat a meal, yet he chose to eat spaghetti on a first date. Now that is confidence! The evening was perfect, even with others watching. There are always eyes on a person sitting in a wheelchair. Why would that be any different?

It was a memorable first date. We all enjoyed the dinner and concert. Before they dropped me off, our friends gave us a moment for a quick goodbye kiss. Brandon doesn't care if I am the one that bends down to kiss him. He would if he could. He more than meets me half way. After the first date, I took over as driver on the rest of our outings. It wasn't impossible to date in a wheelchair; it just took a bit more planning.

Brandon remembers the cute dress that I wore. I remember how special I felt that he wanted so much to take me on a date that he would let others watch and witness something so personal. Our friends remember how blessed they were to be with us and what an honor it was to share our joy.

7.

Taking a Break

After months of dating Brandon, My life seemed out of control. I couldn't help wondering what on earth I was doing. I had more questions than answers, and I desperately needed to get away to think. I was dating a man with special needs. Did I really know what that meant? In the beginning, relationships are exciting and new. As they mature, the newness wears off. Would I still value my relationship with Brandon? Or would I soon find caring for him a drain—both physically and emotionally? These were important questions. This was new to me, but it was just Brandon's usual life. He already had developed his coping skills. Mine were yet to come. After all, we were only nineteen years old.

My family was in Venezuela, oblivious to everything. They had been busy reorganizing their own lives in a strange environment. I kept deceiving myself by saying that I couldn't afford to call them very often. The truth was that I didn't want to deal with their questions yet. I had enough of my own.

My friends and I took a little road trip just to get away. There is nothing like the banter of young women and retail therapy to mask reality. It did just that. We stayed with a friend in Salt Lake City. It helped me step back so I could take a look at my life.

But my trip left Brandon with questions of his own. He wondered if I would bail on him, just as others had, and whether he was as important to me as I was to him. He couldn't wait for my return to get answers. So he called my apartment and left me a message—three messages, actually, to fit all he had to say on the answering machine. He was honest and genuine and an open book.

He told me in many ways how much he cared about me. He expressed his love and said that he could see us spending the rest of our lives together. It was the first time I had heard him say that he loved me. It took me minutes before I could hear the rest of the message. Didn't he just say that he loved me? He wanted someone to love him as much as he loved me, and he thought he had found that. He could see himself married to me.

I played his messages over and over. I felt his love and determination to do everything he could to make this relationship work. It was the first time I allowed myself to realize that I was, in fact, in love. We were in love. I couldn't wait to see him so that he could say those three little words in person. I hurried over to his house. It was clear that I missed him as much as he missed me. Neither of us could deny our feelings for one another, and neither of us had ever had such a relationship.

I told him that I couldn't imagine my life without him. I knelt by his wheelchair so that he could hold me. We kissed, gently, for what seemed like hours. It was so good to be near him. Our feelings for one another were clear. Over and over we both just whispered, "I love you, I love you."

Now what? I wondered as I drove myself back home.

I needed to go to Venezuela for Christmas to see my family. It felt like I had known Brandon forever, but the truth was, I had just met him in October. How could life change so fast?

I went one last time to see Brandon before I left for Venezuela. He gave me the most beautiful ruby and diamond ring for Christmas. He called it a friendship ring. I was overjoyed! But my joy would be short-lived. My family was not happy, and clearly, I had some explaining to do.

8.

Christmas in Venezuela

When I broke the news, my family was less than pleased. It was an unusual Christmas to begin with, and then I showed up with a new life and a friendship ring.

The questions were immediate and endless.

"How disabled is he?"

"How could this happen so fast?"

"You are planning to finish school first, aren't you?"

"The ring is just a friendship ring, right?"

"He will finish school too, won't he?"

"How will he make a living?"

"How can you afford to marry?"

"How will you take care of him?"

"Where will you live?"

"You could very well have to be the bread winner. Have you thought of that?"

"What if Brandon needs hospitalizations? How will you pay for it?"

"Is this a genetic disease? Could you pass it on to children?"

"Do you love him? How could you fall in love with a disabled man?"

"You are only nineteen years old. How old is he?"

"Have you met his family? Are you from the same faith?"

"What on earth are you thinking?"

My three sisters and parents were firing questions faster than I could answer.

No matter how hard I tried to ease their discomfort, it was not possible. They insisted that I finish college first, let the relationship cool, and then take another look after graduation. They forbade me to marry before I'd finished school.

I listened, but I was already in love. My parents had married young, against everyone's wishes. I had questions of my own to ask them. Why were they judging me when we hadn't even formally discussed marriage? They were still married, despite marrying young. Didn't every marriage have obstacles? But my parents insisted that we had more than obstacles—we would have hurdles!

Brandon's entire life had hurdles. He met each one fearlessly and came out better for having been through them. He started each day optimistic and happy for a new chance to live another day. He held me up, not the other way around. I was his physical strength, and he was my rock. His emotional strength was endless. It came from faith in God and the courage he had earned from struggle. He was the most forgiving person that I had ever met. He didn't even know how to hold a grudge. I wished my parents could have known these things about him like I did.

In spite of the bomb I'd dropped, my family did have a positive Christmas holiday. We were not familiar with a warm Christmas, but we enjoyed it anyway. We loved the palm trees laced in lights and our Christmas tree with clay ornaments. Shorts and sandals instead of boots and layers were strange. Sand instead of snow was even stranger. We all agreed that it was a good kind of strange.

Mom made Gouda macaroni and cheese. It was impossible to do a traditional Christmas dinner. We weren't able to find some of the foods for our holiday meal. Venezuela was anything but traditional. This was the first time that my father had taken a job out of the country. It was a new experience for all of us.

My parents relaxed after their initial shock concerning Brandon. I think they thought that they had doused the fire and that there would be no wedding soon. They just didn't understand. It was too late and I was in too deep.

I went back to my life in Utah, and they went on with theirs. I wished that they were more understanding. I prayed hard that someday we would reach an agreement and that they would see Brandon as I saw him.

9.

Starting a Career

Brandon has this incredible mind and spirit, combined with enormous amounts of energy, and he is trapped in an unwilling body. He had to figure out what he could do to make a living. He was getting married soon, and time was flying.

His church gathered about three hundred people to fast and pray for his employment, and within a week, Brandon found a job. He saw an ad in the newspaper that said, "If you can talk your way out of any situation and can think on your feet, apply here." That was Brandon.

He started working right away. The office was on the second floor of the building and was not handicapped accessible, so two men had to carry him and his wheelchair up the stairs every day. First they carried Brandon and plopped him down in a chair. Then they carried the wheelchair, which weighs several hundred pounds, up the staircase and helped him back in it. He went through that same ritual everyday to go home. It was not the way he wanted to go to and from work, but he could do it. He wanted a life with me more, and he could swallow his pride.

He would be trained to be an investigator and would be an asset locator. An asset locator is a person who looks for hidden money when people are claiming not to have any. When a doctor has patients who say they don't have money to pay for the services, sometimes searching is necessary to locate their funds. Attorneys need this service as well. Brandon quickly found an easier and more efficient way to do this. He reorganized their system.

I quit school and got a job there as well. Together we started noticing that our new boss was doing unscrupulous things. He started working for tabloids without even thinking of the consequences that it would cause others. Brandon and I had to rethink our job choice. We couldn't work for someone who didn't share our values.

We knew we had made the right choice to leave after our boss duct taped Brandon to his wheelchair to make fun of him for being handicapped in front of other employees. We had to get out of there quick. We had never seen such a horrifying thing happen to anyone! Brandon has endured much in his young life. Here was just another example of humiliation.

As it turned out, our boss announced that he would be moving his business to Montana, and we knew Brandon could not endure the climate there, so it was the perfect time to leave. Once again, we prayed for guidance. We borrowed $5,000 from a very trusting banker using Brandon's van as collateral to start our business, and we were on our way. We were both trained as asset locators, so we knew the business and had contacts for clients. We could actually work out of Brandon's home until we got married and had a home of our own. It was the perfect job for Brandon. He didn't have to leave home to go to work.

That $5,000 we borrowed ran out quickly before we started getting paid from our clients. We struggled briefly trying to stay afloat. Once again we prayed together. The next day we found a check in the mail that we hadn't expected for $1,000 from the government. It was enough for us to get by until our payments from our clients started coming. We have been successful ever since.

10.

Planning a Wedding

This was clearly not going to be a grandiose wedding, but it would still be my fairy tale. We didn't have the money for a large affair. I was going to marry the love of my life, and Brandon would be marrying his. My family was adamant about me finishing college first, though, and wouldn't talk about a wedding yet.

Brandon had called my dad in Venezuela three times to beg for his blessing. My dad forbade the wedding and wouldn't even discuss it. Clearly my parents' fears were their focus. They couldn't see how our marriage would survive. They advised me many times to break it off. In time, they told me, my heart and Brandon's would heal. It was better to let go now, they thought.

Brandon wouldn't hear of it. He reminded me daily that we had each other. That was a lot more than many other people ever had. We were old enough to make our own decisions. We would make a run for it. Las Vegas was close and had weddings by the minute. We would stay in a hotel and have a mini honeymoon.

It took several days to plan. We knew we wanted to be together. I had to believe that someday, my family would love Brandon, as soon as they got to know him. They would see what I see in him. *It's better to ask for forgiveness than permission,* as the saying goes, so we just wouldn't tell them our plans. We'd call them after the wedding.

Brandon's family had their concerns, but they loved both of us. Kathy, Brandon's mother, suspected and feared that we would run off to get married. She wanted the loving arms of the family wrapped around us on such a special day. She told us how important is was to have the support of our church family.

We had the van packed and were about to leave when Kathy came running up to us to plead one more time for us to get married at home. She would help in any way she could. We could plan, arrange, and get married in our family ward at our church house in one week.

We saw the emotion in Brandon's mother's face and the tears streaming down her cheeks. They had been through so many unhappy moments in Brandon's life that they wanted to be a part of this very joyous time.

We agreed, unpacked the car, and started the whirlwind wedding planning. During this time, Kathy taught me how to physically care for Brandon. He has use of his limbs, but his muscles are not strong enough for him to walk or even stand. Brandon would need help with even the smallest of tasks. The things I do automatically, and totally take for granted are difficult for him. He needed help brushing his teeth, shaving, combing his hair, and even getting a drink of water. I would need to help him dress and undress. He needed someone else's strength to get in and out of bed. While Kathy was teaching me, Brandon often turned away or buried his face in his arm. Who wants their fiancé to see them in that vulnerable position?

There were little things that I hadn't even thought of yet. Through all of Kathy's instruction, I couldn't help wondering if I was even capable of taking care of him. *But doesn't everyone do all that they can for the ones they love?* I concluded. The only difference for me was that there would be more to do. I felt honored that God would entrust me with Brandon's care, just as He had entrusted Kathy all these years.

I knew my husband would require a lot of care, but I hadn't realize how much physical and emotional strength it would take to complete these tasks. Brandon was so patient with me. Once again he had to swallow his pride and mask his dignity for me to learn some of the care. It was a trade-off for him, and he thought that getting me was worth it.

I rented a wedding dress. Not one of the elegant works of art that you would find in a bride's magazine. It was just someone else's dress, and I would make it work. I wanted Brandon more. It wasn't about the dress, really. It was about a relationship. It was about finding someone who loved me for who I am. I was about to become Brandon Thornley's wife, and I was so excited. I loved him more than life itself.

Brandon's mother planned a dinner with close friends and family for after the ceremony. It would be a small wedding and reception, as it should be. I never wanted a lavish wedding anyway. I wanted to be surrounded by people who were important to us. We invited people who loved and supported us. An intimate gathering would be perfect.

My prince arrived in a wheelchair. He couldn't have been more handsome or charming if he had arrived on a white horse. Brandon's mom and sister helped me with my hair, makeup, and getting into my gown.

My sisters and parents didn't know about the wedding and were not going to be with me. There would be no familiar giggles with sisters as I prepared for the most important day of my life. They would not be my bridesmaids scrambling into their dresses. My father would not be giving me away. I missed my family enormously and the moments we would have shared forever.

But life has its tradeoffs. I was getting the life partner I wanted and so was he. We would be forever together. Just as I had thought, I wasn't going to let it be about the dress or formalities. I didn't even think about what I was wearing. I only thought about how happy I felt inside.

We were promising our hearts, souls, and lives to each other forever. I knew we would have better and richer lives together than we ever would have apart. It was the best day of our lives and one that we will forever remember.

We have very few photographs of that day. We didn't need more. It was imprinted in our hearts and minds. For better or worse, on October 28, 1995, in our church house, we were pronounced Mr. and Mrs. Brandon Thornley. As Matthew 19:6 says, "What God has joined together, let no man put asunder." Amen.

11.

Honeymoon

We were one. Nothing and no one could stop us now. We could not afford much time off from work. It would be life as usual. We would have to take moments wherever we could find them to be alone together. We lived in Brandon's family's home. There were always eyes on us. We were getting very creative at finding places where we could be alone.

We spent one night at Sherwood Hills. It was the first time that I got to put Brandon's mother's training into practice. I tried to put Brandon in a lift to lower him into the whirlpool tub and almost ended our brief one-day marriage by drowning my new husband! I quickly realized that I would need a bit more training. It gives us something to laugh about on each anniversary. We loved being together. I felt honored that God had brought us together, and I was thankful that Kathy, Brandon's mother, gave me caregiving instructions. I would need remedial classes soon, or Brandon would have to take some form of instruction just to survive my caregiving!

The reality of it all set in soon. There would be no dividing of household chores ever. Even though I knew that coming in to this marriage, it was very real now. We were blessed that Brandon could make a living for us. I would need to do everything else, and everything was a lot.

In spite of Kathy's training, there was more to do than I thought, but I adored him, so I was ready. Some days were overwhelming. We were determined that we would do this by ourselves. We wouldn't ask anyone for help. We were in with both feet and our eyes open. No rose-colored glasses for us.

Each day started early, with my grooming and Brandon's grooming. I didn't realize how much time that it would take. Brandon was so patient and anticipated the problems we would have. He'd had to rely on others his entire life. This time it was the love of his life helping. He hated watching his new bride struggle. The first few years were hard. It was much more difficult than I had realized. Kathy had made it look so easy. Our days were long and stressful.

Brandon needed help rolling over, three times every night. Some nights it seemed I would just get to sleep and it would be time to help him turn. It hurt him to have to wake me up. I couldn't get a good night's sleep. At one point, I was so discouraged (and didn't want Brandon to know how I felt) that I had to leave the room to cry. With my face buried in my hands, my body trembling, and the tears flowing, I heard God speaking to me. He told me that I could do this and that it would be all right. From that point on, I gathered more strength and things became easier. I wasn't alone.

We could fall asleep holding one another and wake up holding one another. I loved feeling his breath on my face and feeling the warmth of his arms around me. The benefits would outweigh the problems. Our bond was getting stronger by the day. We loved being together.

$$12.$$

Meeting My Parents

My parents hadn't ever thought that the man I would fall in love with would be disabled. I hadn't ever really thought about that either. They hadn't warmed up to the idea of our marriage. It certainly wasn't a dream that they had for their oldest daughter. I was still their first daughter to wed.

They had dreams for me, as all parents do, but I was not fulfilling many of them. I had a great childhood, but we were not brought up in the church, and they were not LDS. They did not understand my newly found faith. They expected me to go through a time period of questioning and learning about life, my direction, and who I am, but not every young woman finds some of the answers in marrying a disabled man and devoting her life to a religion that they didn't understand. They were puzzled that their daughter would choose this. Was she still the daughter that they knew and loved?

I hadn't anticipated the consequences of leaving the nest with no faith. To me, it was like being capsized in the ocean with no life preserver. You can only tread for a short while, and then you need to grab onto something that will save your life. That was what my faith was to me. It was a life preserver when I desperately needed it.

This marriage was God's plan. This plan was in place before our births. Brandon and I were meant to be together. We had an unbreakable bond. Didn't God design sex between a man and his wife for that reason? When intimacy is saved for marriage, it seals that unbreakable bond. My mom and dad would just have to see how committed we were to one another.

My dad's job ended in Venezuela, and he and Mom eventually moved back to Utah. They didn't have a home yet, so we invited them to move in with us. I think that was part of God's plan as well. It was a chance for my parents to see our life together and the reality of our marriage.

Every day my parents got to see our routine. They saw how much we loved one another and how we truly loved being together. They could see how hard Brandon worked to provide for us. Their fears diminished.

They were able to see that Brandon was the head of our household. He showed them every day just how much he appreciated me and our life together. He gave everything he had and more to make our relationship work.

My mom loved debating politics with Brandon. She saw just how knowledgeable he is and appreciated his conservative views. Why was there ever a stereotype that disabled people are not smart? Brandon needed to prove just how intelligent he is. He was used to proving himself to others.

Mom started helping with his caregiving. Eventually, my parents began to understand how lasting our love was. They came to know the Brandon that I know. They were able to see that I was still the daughter that they knew and loved but that I was now more complete and happier than I had ever been.

Today, they love Brandon as one of their own. My mom even designed and made a strap that helps him sit upright in the wheelchair. She makes him slippers. She prepares his favorite foods. He was heart-broken when they decided to take another job out of the country. We are blessed to have an extended family that loves and supports us. My family is now his family forever, too

13.

Life Today

Brandon and I live a full life. We are together most of the time. Brandon seldom has a bad day, and he doesn't spend his time indulging in self-pity. His philosophy is that the only real handicap is having a closed mind—that "If you think you can't, you are probably right!"

Brandon wakes up knowing each day is a blessing. We settle each misunderstanding right away so that we don't waste any of our precious time together. We are so thankful that we have found one another.

Brandon works out of our home running our business. He is the provider for both of us. I run our household and take care of Brandon's needs. Together we are enough and have all that we need.

We have made the decision not to have children. We know just how much care Brandon needs and we were afraid that we would not have the time necessary for the care and needs of children.

We live in a new stucco house that is handicapped accessible. It is all that I dreamed a house could be. Together we have made it a home. It is warm and inviting, and the door is always open to our friends and family. We share our lives and our home with our rambunctious Shih Tzu Bentley, and our new Shih Tzu puppy Mini Cooper, who always make us laugh. They show us new ways to love everything and everyone. They are the first greeters at our door.

Our puppy, Mini Cooper, has recently been diagnosed with cancer and is undergoing chemotherapy. How can a four-month old puppy have cancer? Once again, we have drawn on our faith and are doing all we can to help our puppy survive this disease. Life will always have struggles and lessons to learn.

It was by no coincidence that I met Brandon Thornley. He has taught me patience, humility, and how to live every day to the fullest. He tells me daily just how much he loves me and how beautiful he thinks I am. He writes me letters filled with love and devotion. He is grateful for everything that I do for him.

Brandon will never be able to open a door for me or pull out my chair or make me dinner. He won't be pulling weeds from our garden or mowing our lawn. But you will sometimes find him sitting outside, keeping me company, with his face to the sun, smiling and enjoying our time together and thankful for another beautiful day.

You won't find him feeling sorry for what he doesn't have or cannot do. He is honestly happy with what he has been given. Isn't that what is important, being grateful for what you have?

With each day, we have new challenges. Brandon will continue to lose mobility as he ages. He remains strong in his faith and love of God and knows that he is never alone. Our love and devotion to one another gets stronger. We are married, and in every sense, we are truly one. We are one body and one mind. I am his arms and legs, and he is my strength and the love of my life. We have weathered each storm together.

We have a loving support system from our LDS community and supportive extended family. We are truly blessed to have many friends. We have always had a life of abundance.

We enjoy travel, and Brandon especially loves cruises. We hope to travel more in the future. We have a list of places that we hope to go. We love board games, taking walks together, eating out, playing games on the computer, and entertaining friends and family. We count our blessings every day.

Brandon's LDS faith doesn't waver. He believes that we each have a purpose. I am thankful that Brandon had the strength and courage to reach out to find his. On that one fall day sixteen years ago, Brandon said a prayer for direction and found my name. With a simple click, we were pioneers of the Internet matching-making future, and we were forever connected and our lives forever changed. We are inseparable.

In our LDS faith, we are sealed for an eternity. We were sealed on August 1, 1998 in the Logan Temple. We will be married forever. We look forward to that time when Brandon's body is whole and we can walk hand in hand together. Our earthly time is so brief. We can see beyond to our heavenly future.

I guess I would say that we had the courage to to live our own fairy tale romance

Can I tell you a story? Once upon a time, there was a young woman who knew that if she moved to Utah, she would meet someone who would change her life. While sitting at a computer in the library one day, magically a message appeared. She wept as she read. The honesty of the words touched her soul. She knew this was more than a message. It would change her life forever. She would find love and a bond that could never be broken. For you see, that young woman was me. I had mail from Brandon Thornley.

This is one of my favorite letters from Brandon. He continues to write out his feelings for me. I am so blessed!

My Dearest Hillary:

I thought of getting you a card from the store, but I knew it wouldn't do you justice. I also pondered getting you some flowers, then I decided giving you a piece of my heart might be a bit more appropriate.

When I think of all the precious things in this world; jewelry, houses, newborn babies, a sunset in July and many others, I know they pale in comparison to my one true love. I have often thought of how I could put my feelings for you into words, but it cannot be done. Maybe in the life to come that will be possible, but not in this world.

I look at you on a daily basis and marvel. How could one so very young be so brave, so much more mature beyond her years and so Christ-like? I have met only one other person like you in my life, that being my own mother. I often wonder how you do so many things; how do you forgive me so many countless times; how do you care for another person so wonderfully, and how are you so unselfish??? These questions often come to my mind.

You are a very selfless person, Hillary. I know how much you sacrifice for me, for us, for the best. I do appreciate you oh so much. I only wish I could show you. Sometimes I am very troubled. It seems like there is nothing but despair. I only need to think 'Hill loves me' and it makes it feel a bit better.

It has been a rough 2 ½ years. Heck, it was rough before we got married! When we say "yes" at the temple, there will be tears of joy. I do love you with all that I am. You have saved me in many countless ways. I truly have married a gem. You are perfect for me.

On this special day, I wish you the happiest of birthdays and want you to know the Bran you talked to for hours on end at night, the Bran that held you till he was numb, and the Bran that made love to his beautiful wife, is yours forever. June 3rd is the greatest day I have known. The day that you were born is the day the Heavenly Father gave me a piece of my heart that was missing.

I love you Hillary M. Thornley!! Have a wonderful birthday!!

Always and forever,

Your husband and eternal companion,
Brandon

August 24, 1998

Dear Brandon and Hillary,

After serving 20 months as your bishop, I leave this ward with many memories that tug at my heart and open my tear ducts.   One of the highlights of my time as bishop was your sealing for time and all eternity in the temple of our God. What an outpouring of the Spirit. Not a dry eye! I know that Lord is well pleased with your decision ... and I could feel the joy expressed by your family ... and I even sensed the presence of some who have gone beyond.

Now that I've been called to a new arena for service, my hope is that you would give your complete support to Bishop Ringle and do your part to fulfill the scripture:

> *Be ye kind one to another, tenderhearted,*
> *forgiving one another, even as God for Christ's*
> *sake hath forgiven you.*
>
> *-- Ephesians 4:32*

May God bless and keep you until we join together in that ultimate "Caring Community" ... in the Celestial Kingdom with the Father and the Son and all the Saints.

With all my heart,

E. Jeffrey Hill
Bishop, Logan 10th Ward
1996-1998